50 Japanese Dessert Recipes for Home

By: Kelly Johnson

Table of Contents

- Mochi Ice Cream
- Dorayaki (Red Bean Pancakes)
- Matcha Green Tea Ice Cream
- Taiyaki (Fish-shaped Pancakes)
- Anmitsu (Fruit Jelly Dessert)
- Wagashi (Traditional Japanese Confections)
- Mitarashi Dango (Grilled Rice Dumplings with Sweet Soy Sauce)
- Sakura Mochi (Cherry Blossom Rice Cake)
- Yokan (Sweet Bean Jelly)
- Green Tea Tiramisu
- Kuzumochi (Arrowroot Starch Cake)
- Castella (Japanese Sponge Cake)
- Ichigo Daifuku (Strawberry Mochi)
- Warabi Mochi (Bracken Starch Dumplings)
- Uiro (Steamed Rice Cake)
- Matcha Cheesecake
- Yatsuhashi (Cinnamon-flavored Rice Cake)
- Hanami Dango (Tri-colored Dumplings)
- Kintsuba (Sweet Bean Paste Cake)
- Kinako Mochi (Roasted Soybean Flour Rice Cake)
- Sakura Anpan (Cherry Blossom Sweet Bun)
- Sata Andagi (Okinawan Doughnuts)
- Karukan (Sweet Potato Cake)
- Mitarashi Kushi Dango (Skewered Rice Dumplings with Sweet Soy Sauce)
- Kuri Kinton (Candied Sweet Potatoes with Chestnuts)
- Momiji Manju (Maple Leaf-shaped Cake with Sweet Bean Paste)
- Amazake (Sweet Fermented Rice Drink)
- Kasutera (Japanese Honey Castella Cake)
- Senbei (Rice Crackers)
- Kuri Mochi (Chestnut Rice Cake)
- Shiratama Dango (Rice Dumplings)
- Hishi Mochi (Diamond-shaped Rice Cakes)
- Mizu Yokan (Water Yokan)
- Yubeshi (Citrus-flavored Rice Cake)
- Kuri Anmitsu (Chestnut Jelly Dessert)

- Kuzumanju (Steamed Wheat Cake)
- Goma Dango (Sesame Dumplings)
- Yomogi Mochi (Japanese Mugwort Rice Cake)
- Hanabiramochi (Cherry Blossom Rice Cake)
- Kusa Mochi (Grass-flavored Rice Cake)
- Wasanbon (Refined Japanese Sugar)
- Kinako Warabi Mochi (Roasted Soybean Flour Bracken Starch Dumplings)
- Kusa Dango (Grass-flavored Dumplings)
- Yuzu Marmalade
- Akafuku Mochi (Red Bean Paste-covered Rice Cake)
- Mizuame (Sweet Rice Syrup)
- Kudzu Mochi (Arrowroot Starch Cake)
- Yomogi Dango (Japanese Mugwort Dumplings)
- Kibi Dango (Millet Dumplings)
- Amazake Ice Cream

Mochi Ice Cream

Ingredients:

- Your favorite flavors of ice cream
- 1 cup (150g) mochiko (sweet rice flour)
- 1/4 cup (50g) granulated sugar
- 3/4 cup (180ml) water
- Potato starch or cornstarch, for dusting

Instructions:

1. Let your ice cream soften slightly at room temperature until it's easy to scoop but not melted.
2. Line a baking sheet with parchment paper or wax paper. Scoop small balls of ice cream (about 1 tablespoon each) onto the prepared baking sheet. Place the baking sheet in the freezer and freeze the ice cream balls until firm, about 1-2 hours.
3. In a microwave-safe bowl, combine the mochiko (sweet rice flour) and granulated sugar. Gradually stir in the water until smooth.
4. Microwave the mochi mixture on high for 1 minute. Remove from the microwave and stir well.
5. Return the mochi mixture to the microwave and microwave for an additional 1-2 minutes, stirring every 30 seconds, until the mixture becomes thick and sticky.
6. Let the mochi dough cool slightly until it's cool enough to handle but still pliable.
7. Dust a clean work surface with potato starch or cornstarch to prevent sticking. Place a small portion of the mochi dough on the dusted surface and flatten it into a thin circle.
8. Place one of the frozen ice cream balls in the center of the mochi circle. Gently wrap the mochi dough around the ice cream ball, pinching and twisting the edges to seal it completely.
9. Repeat the process with the remaining ice cream balls and mochi dough.
10. Place the mochi-covered ice cream balls back on the baking sheet and freeze until firm, about 1-2 hours.
11. Once the mochi ice cream balls are frozen solid, they are ready to serve. Enjoy these delicious treats as a refreshing dessert or snack!

You can also experiment with different flavors of ice cream and add-ins for endless variations of mochi ice cream. Enjoy making and indulging in these delightful Japanese-inspired treats!

Dorayaki (Red Bean Pancakes)

Ingredients:

For the pancakes:

- 2 large eggs
- 1/2 cup (100g) granulated sugar
- 1 tablespoon honey
- 1 teaspoon vanilla extract
- 1 cup (120g) all-purpose flour
- 1/2 teaspoon baking powder
- Pinch of salt
- 2-3 tablespoons milk (if needed)

For the red bean filling:

- 1 cup (200g) cooked sweet red bean paste (anko)

Instructions:

1. In a mixing bowl, whisk together the eggs and granulated sugar until pale and fluffy.
2. Add the honey and vanilla extract to the egg mixture and whisk until well combined.
3. Sift the all-purpose flour, baking powder, and salt into the egg mixture. Gently fold the dry ingredients into the wet ingredients until just combined. Be careful not to overmix, as this can result in tough pancakes.
4. If the batter seems too thick, you can add 2-3 tablespoons of milk to achieve a smoother consistency. The batter should be thick but still pourable.
5. Heat a non-stick skillet or griddle over medium heat. Lightly grease the surface with butter or cooking spray.
6. Spoon about 2 tablespoons of batter onto the skillet to form each pancake. Cook until bubbles form on the surface of the pancakes and the edges begin to set, about 2-3 minutes.
7. Carefully flip the pancakes and cook for an additional 1-2 minutes, or until golden brown and cooked through.

8. Remove the pancakes from the skillet and let them cool slightly on a wire rack.
9. Once the pancakes are cool enough to handle, spread a spoonful of sweet red bean paste (anko) onto the center of one pancake.
10. Place another pancake on top of the red bean paste to create a sandwich.
11. Repeat the process with the remaining pancakes and red bean paste.
12. Serve the dorayaki immediately, or store them in an airtight container at room temperature for up to 1-2 days.

Enjoy these homemade dorayaki as a delightful snack or dessert, perfect for enjoying with a cup of tea or coffee!

Matcha Green Tea Ice Cream

Ingredients:

- 2 cups (480ml) heavy cream
- 1 cup (240ml) whole milk
- 1/2 cup (100g) granulated sugar
- 3 tablespoons (15g) matcha green tea powder
- 4 large egg yolks
- Pinch of salt

Instructions:

1. In a saucepan, combine the heavy cream, whole milk, and granulated sugar over medium heat. Heat the mixture, stirring occasionally, until the sugar is dissolved and the mixture is just beginning to steam. Do not let it boil.
2. In a small bowl, whisk the matcha green tea powder with a small amount of hot water to form a smooth paste. Add a little more water if needed to achieve a smooth consistency.
3. In a separate bowl, whisk the egg yolks until smooth.
4. Gradually pour a small amount of the hot cream mixture into the egg yolks, whisking constantly, to temper the eggs. Continue adding the hot cream mixture slowly, whisking constantly, until about half of the cream mixture has been incorporated into the eggs.
5. Pour the tempered egg mixture back into the saucepan with the remaining cream mixture, whisking constantly to combine.
6. Cook the mixture over medium heat, stirring constantly, until it thickens slightly and coats the back of a spoon, about 5-7 minutes. Do not let it boil.
7. Remove the saucepan from heat and strain the mixture through a fine-mesh sieve into a clean bowl to remove any lumps.
8. Whisk the matcha green tea paste into the strained custard until well combined.
9. Cover the bowl with plastic wrap, pressing it directly onto the surface of the custard to prevent a skin from forming. Refrigerate the custard until completely chilled, preferably overnight.
10. Once the custard is chilled, churn it in an ice cream maker according to the manufacturer's instructions until it reaches a soft-serve consistency.
11. Transfer the churned ice cream to a freezer-safe container and freeze for at least 4 hours, or until firm.
12. Serve the matcha green tea ice cream scooped into bowls or cones, and enjoy!

This homemade matcha green tea ice cream is creamy, flavorful, and perfect for enjoying as a refreshing dessert or snack. Enjoy the unique taste of matcha in every creamy bite!

Taiyaki (Fish-shaped Pancakes)

Ingredients:

For the taiyaki batter:

- 1 cup (120g) all-purpose flour
- 1 tablespoon cornstarch
- 1/4 cup (50g) granulated sugar
- 1 teaspoon baking powder
- Pinch of salt
- 1 large egg
- 3/4 cup (180ml) whole milk
- 1 teaspoon vanilla extract
- 2 tablespoons (30g) unsalted butter, melted

For the filling:

- Sweet red bean paste (anko)
- Custard
- Chocolate spread
- Nutella
- Your choice of filling

Instructions:

1. In a large mixing bowl, whisk together the all-purpose flour, cornstarch, granulated sugar, baking powder, and salt.
2. In a separate bowl, whisk together the egg, whole milk, vanilla extract, and melted butter until well combined.
3. Gradually pour the wet ingredients into the dry ingredients, whisking until you have a smooth batter. Be careful not to overmix.
4. Preheat your taiyaki maker or fish-shaped waffle iron according to the manufacturer's instructions.
5. Lightly grease the molds of the taiyaki maker with cooking spray or brush with oil.
6. Pour a small amount of batter into each mold, filling it about halfway.
7. Add your desired filling to one side of each fish-shaped mold. You can use sweet red bean paste, custard, chocolate spread, Nutella, or any other filling you like.
8. Spoon a little more batter over the filling to cover it completely.

9. Close the taiyaki maker and cook for 2-3 minutes, or until the taiyaki are golden brown and crispy.
10. Carefully remove the taiyaki from the maker and transfer them to a wire rack to cool slightly before serving.
11. Repeat the process with the remaining batter and filling until all the taiyaki are cooked.
12. Serve the taiyaki warm and enjoy as a delicious snack or dessert!

Taiyaki is best enjoyed fresh and warm, but you can also store any leftovers in an airtight container and reheat them in a toaster oven or microwave before serving. Enjoy these adorable fish-shaped pancakes filled with your favorite sweet fillings!

Anmitsu (Fruit Jelly Dessert)

Ingredients:

For the agar jelly:

- 4 cups (960ml) water
- 2 teaspoons agar agar powder
- 1/2 cup (100g) granulated sugar

For the sweet red bean paste (anko):

- 1 cup (200g) cooked sweet red beans (azuki beans)
- 1/2 cup (100g) granulated sugar
- 1/4 cup (60ml) water

For the syrup (mitsu):

- 1/2 cup (120ml) water
- 1/2 cup (100g) granulated sugar
- 1 tablespoon honey
- 1 tablespoon mirin (Japanese sweet rice wine)
- 1 teaspoon vanilla extract

For serving:

- Assorted fruits (such as strawberries, kiwi, orange segments, and canned fruit cocktail)
- Shiratama dango (small rice flour dumplings), optional
- Sweetened condensed milk, optional
- Ice cream, optional

Instructions:

1. Start by preparing the agar jelly. In a saucepan, combine the water, agar agar powder, and granulated sugar. Stir well to dissolve the sugar and agar agar powder.

2. Bring the mixture to a boil over medium heat, stirring constantly. Once it boils, reduce the heat to low and simmer for 2-3 minutes, continuing to stir.
3. Remove the saucepan from the heat and pour the agar jelly mixture into a square or rectangular dish. Let it cool to room temperature, then refrigerate until set, about 1-2 hours.
4. While the agar jelly is setting, prepare the sweet red bean paste (anko). In a small saucepan, combine the cooked sweet red beans, granulated sugar, and water. Cook over medium heat, stirring frequently, until the mixture thickens to a paste-like consistency, about 10-15 minutes. Remove from heat and let it cool.
5. Prepare the syrup (mitsu) by combining water, granulated sugar, honey, mirin, and vanilla extract in a small saucepan. Bring to a simmer over medium heat, stirring occasionally, until the sugar is completely dissolved. Remove from heat and let it cool to room temperature.
6. Once the agar jelly is set, remove it from the refrigerator and cut it into small cubes.
7. Prepare any additional toppings you'd like to include, such as slicing the assorted fruits and cooking shiratama dango according to package instructions.
8. To assemble the Anmitsu, divide the agar jelly cubes, sweet red bean paste, assorted fruits, and shiratama dango (if using) among serving bowls.
9. Drizzle the syrup (mitsu) over the Anmitsu.
10. Optionally, top each serving with a drizzle of sweetened condensed milk or a scoop of ice cream.
11. Serve the Anmitsu immediately and enjoy!

Anmitsu is a refreshing and delightful dessert that combines a variety of textures and flavors. It's perfect for enjoying on a hot day or as a sweet treat after a meal. Feel free to customize the toppings and syrup according to your preferences.

Wagashi (Traditional Japanese Confections)

Ingredients:

- 200g sweet bean paste (anko)
- 100g shiratamako (glutinous rice flour)
- 80ml water
- Food coloring (optional)
- Potato starch or cornstarch (for dusting)

Instructions:

1. Start by preparing the sweet bean paste (anko) if you're making it from scratch, or use store-bought if you prefer.
2. In a mixing bowl, combine the shiratamako (glutinous rice flour) and water. Stir well until a smooth dough forms.
3. Divide the dough into smaller portions if you want to make different colors or flavors of Nerikiri.
4. If using food coloring, add a small amount to each portion of dough and knead until the color is evenly distributed. You can use traditional Japanese colors such as red, green, or yellow, or any color you prefer.
5. Dust your hands and work surface with potato starch or cornstarch to prevent sticking. Take a small portion of the sweet bean paste (anko) and flatten it into a disc.
6. Place a portion of the colored dough on top of the sweet bean paste and gently wrap the paste around the dough, shaping it into your desired shape. You can make simple shapes like balls, or more intricate shapes like flowers or leaves.
7. Repeat the process with the remaining portions of dough and sweet bean paste.
8. Once you've shaped all of the Nerikiri, they are ready to be served. Enjoy them with a cup of green tea for a traditional Japanese treat!

This recipe makes about 10-12 pieces of Nerikiri, depending on the size and shape of each piece. Feel free to experiment with different flavors and colors to create your own unique wagashi.

Mitarashi Dango (Grilled Rice Dumplings with Sweet Soy Sauce)

Ingredients:

For the dango (rice dumplings):

- 1 cup (150g) mochiko (sweet rice flour)
- 1/4 cup (60ml) warm water
- 2-3 tablespoons additional water, as needed

For the sweet soy sauce glaze (mitarashi sauce):

- 1/4 cup (60ml) soy sauce
- 2 tablespoons (30g) granulated sugar
- 1 tablespoon mirin (Japanese sweet rice wine)
- 1 tablespoon water
- 1 teaspoon potato starch or cornstarch, dissolved in 1 tablespoon water

Instructions:

1. Start by making the dango (rice dumplings). In a mixing bowl, combine the mochiko (sweet rice flour) with the warm water. Mix well until a smooth dough forms.
2. If the dough is too dry, gradually add additional water, one tablespoon at a time, until the dough comes together. The dough should be firm and pliable but not sticky.
3. Divide the dough into small pieces and roll each piece into a ball, about 1 inch (2.5 cm) in diameter.
4. Bring a pot of water to a boil over medium heat. Carefully drop the dango balls into the boiling water and cook for about 2-3 minutes, or until they float to the surface.
5. Remove the cooked dango from the pot with a slotted spoon and transfer them to a bowl of cold water to cool. This step helps to firm up the texture of the dango.
6. While the dango is cooling, prepare the sweet soy sauce glaze (mitarashi sauce). In a small saucepan, combine the soy sauce, granulated sugar, mirin, and water. Stir well and bring the mixture to a simmer over medium heat.

7. Once the mixture is simmering, add the dissolved potato starch or cornstarch and water mixture to the saucepan. Stir constantly until the sauce thickens, about 1-2 minutes. Remove from heat and set aside.
8. Thread the cooled dango onto skewers, dividing them evenly among the skewers.
9. Preheat a grill or grill pan over medium heat. Grill the dango skewers for 2-3 minutes on each side, or until lightly browned and slightly crispy.
10. Once the dango is grilled, brush the sweet soy sauce glaze (mitarashi sauce) over the skewers, coating them evenly.
11. Continue to grill the dango skewers for an additional 1-2 minutes on each side, brushing with more glaze as needed, until they are nicely caramelized and glazed.
12. Remove the dango skewers from the grill and serve immediately.

Mitarashi dango is best enjoyed fresh and warm, but you can also serve them at room temperature. They make a delicious sweet treat or dessert, perfect for enjoying on their own or with a cup of green tea. Enjoy!

Sakura Mochi (Cherry Blossom Rice Cake)

Ingredients:

For the sweet red bean paste (anko):

- 1 cup (200g) cooked sweet red beans (azuki beans)
- 1/2 cup (100g) granulated sugar
- 1/4 cup (60ml) water

For the mochi:

- 1 cup (150g) mochiko (sweet rice flour)
- 2 tablespoons granulated sugar
- 3/4 cup (180ml) water
- A few drops of red food coloring (optional)
- Salt
- Pickled cherry blossom leaves (sakura leaves), rinsed and patted dry

Instructions:

1. Start by making the sweet red bean paste (anko). In a small saucepan, combine the cooked sweet red beans, granulated sugar, and water. Cook over medium heat, stirring frequently, until the mixture thickens to a paste-like consistency, about 10-15 minutes. Remove from heat and let it cool.
2. In a microwave-safe bowl, combine the mochiko (sweet rice flour), granulated sugar, water, and a pinch of salt. Mix well until smooth.
3. If using, add a few drops of red food coloring to the mochi batter and mix until evenly colored.
4. Cover the bowl loosely with plastic wrap and microwave on high for 2-3 minutes, or until the mochi dough is cooked and translucent, stirring halfway through.
5. Dust a clean work surface with potato starch or cornstarch to prevent sticking. Transfer the cooked mochi dough to the dusted surface.
6. Divide the mochi dough into equal portions and shape each portion into a small disk.
7. Place a small amount of sweet red bean paste in the center of each mochi disk.

8. Fold the edges of the mochi over the filling to enclose it completely, shaping it into a round or oval shape.
9. Wrap each mochi ball with a pickled cherry blossom leaf, with the pink side facing outwards.
10. Repeat the process with the remaining mochi dough and sweet red bean paste.
11. Serve the Sakura Mochi immediately, or store them in an airtight container in the refrigerator until ready to serve.

Sakura mochi is a delightful springtime treat with a subtle cherry blossom flavor. Enjoy these delicate and fragrant sweets as a snack or dessert, and savor the flavors of Japanese tradition!

Yokan (Sweet Bean Jelly)

Ingredients:

- 400g sweet red bean paste (anko)
- 10g powdered agar agar (kanten)
- 700ml water
- 100g granulated sugar
- Pinch of salt
- Optional: roasted nuts, cooked chestnuts, or candied fruits for added texture

Instructions:

1. If you're using powdered agar agar, soak it in cold water for about 30 minutes to soften. If you're using agar agar flakes, follow the package instructions for preparation.
2. In a saucepan, combine the soaked agar agar (if using powdered) or agar agar flakes with water. Bring to a boil over medium heat, stirring constantly to dissolve the agar agar completely.
3. Once the agar agar is fully dissolved, reduce the heat to low and add the sweet red bean paste (anko) to the saucepan. Stir well until the anko is fully incorporated into the mixture.
4. Add the granulated sugar and a pinch of salt to the saucepan. Stir until the sugar is completely dissolved.
5. If you're adding any additional ingredients such as roasted nuts, cooked chestnuts, or candied fruits, fold them into the mixture at this point.
6. Remove the saucepan from heat and pour the yokan mixture into a rectangular or square mold lined with plastic wrap. Smooth the top with a spatula or spoon.
7. Let the yokan cool to room temperature, then refrigerate for at least 2-3 hours, or until set firm.
8. Once the yokan is set, remove it from the mold and cut it into individual serving slices.
9. Serve the yokan chilled and enjoy as a traditional Japanese dessert.

Yokan can be stored in an airtight container in the refrigerator for up to several days.

Enjoy its smooth and slightly chewy texture, along with the rich flavor of sweet red bean paste!

Green Tea Tiramisu

Ingredients:

- 1 cup (240ml) heavy cream
- 8 ounces (225g) mascarpone cheese, softened
- 1/2 cup (100g) granulated sugar
- 2 tablespoons matcha green tea powder
- 1 cup (240ml) hot water
- 2 tablespoons matcha green tea powder (for soaking)
- 2 tablespoons granulated sugar (for soaking)
- 2 tablespoons rum or brandy (optional)
- Ladyfinger cookies (savoiardi)
- Cocoa powder, for dusting
- Additional matcha powder, for dusting (optional)
- Matcha Kit Kats or green tea-flavored chocolate, for garnish (optional)

Instructions:

1. In a mixing bowl, whip the heavy cream until stiff peaks form.
2. In a separate bowl, whisk together the mascarpone cheese, granulated sugar, and matcha green tea powder until smooth.
3. Gently fold the whipped cream into the matcha mascarpone mixture until well combined. Set aside.
4. In a shallow dish, combine the hot water, matcha green tea powder, granulated sugar, and rum or brandy (if using) for the soaking liquid. Stir until the sugar and matcha powder are dissolved.
5. Dip each ladyfinger cookie into the matcha soaking liquid for a few seconds, ensuring they are evenly soaked but not overly soggy.
6. Arrange a layer of soaked ladyfinger cookies in the bottom of a serving dish or individual serving glasses.
7. Spread a layer of the matcha mascarpone cream over the soaked ladyfingers.
8. Repeat the layers of soaked ladyfingers and matcha mascarpone cream until you've used up all the ingredients, ending with a layer of the cream on top.
9. Cover the tiramisu with plastic wrap and refrigerate for at least 4 hours, or overnight, to allow the flavors to meld and the dessert to set.
10. Before serving, dust the top of the tiramisu with cocoa powder and additional matcha powder for decoration. Optionally, garnish with Matcha Kit Kats or green tea-flavored chocolate for an extra touch of green tea flavor.

11. Serve the Green Tea Tiramisu chilled and enjoy the delightful fusion of flavors!

This Green Tea Tiramisu is a refreshing and elegant dessert, perfect for any occasion. The subtle bitterness of matcha complements the creamy mascarpone cheese beautifully, creating a unique and unforgettable treat.

Kuzumochi (Arrowroot Starch Cake)

Ingredients:

For the kuzumochi:

- 1 cup (120g) kuzuko (arrowroot starch)
- 1 1/2 cups (360ml) water
- 1/4 cup (50g) granulated sugar
- 1 tablespoon honey
- Optional: 1/2 teaspoon matcha powder (for green tea flavor)

For serving:

- Kuromitsu (black sugar syrup)
- Kinako (roasted soybean flour)

Instructions:

1. In a saucepan, combine the kuzuko (arrowroot starch) and water. Stir well to dissolve the kuzuko completely.
2. Place the saucepan over medium heat and bring the mixture to a simmer, stirring constantly.
3. Once the mixture starts to thicken, add the granulated sugar and honey. Continue to cook and stir until the mixture becomes translucent and reaches a pudding-like consistency.
4. If you want to make matcha-flavored kuzumochi, you can add matcha powder to the mixture at this point and stir until well combined.
5. Remove the saucepan from the heat and let the kuzumochi mixture cool slightly.
6. While the kuzumochi mixture is still warm, pour it into a square or rectangular dish lined with plastic wrap to prevent sticking. Smooth out the surface with a spatula.
7. Let the kuzumochi cool to room temperature, then refrigerate for at least 1-2 hours, or until set firm.
8. Once the kuzumochi is set, remove it from the refrigerator and cut it into bite-sized pieces.

9. Serve the kuzumochi with a drizzle of kuromitsu (black sugar syrup) and a sprinkle of kinako (roasted soybean flour) on top.
10. Enjoy the kuzumochi chilled as a refreshing and delightful Japanese dessert!

Kuzumochi has a unique texture that is slightly chewy and jelly-like, making it a popular treat, especially during the warmer months. The combination of the sweet syrup and nutty kinako complements the delicate flavor of the arrowroot starch perfectly.

Castella (Japanese Sponge Ca)

Ingredients:

- 6 large eggs, at room temperature
- 1 cup (200g) granulated sugar
- 1 cup (120ml) whole milk
- 1 tablespoon honey
- 1 tablespoon mirin (Japanese sweet rice wine)
- 1 cup (120g) cake flour
- 1 teaspoon baking powder
- Vegetable oil, for greasing
- Optional: sesame seeds for topping

Instructions:

1. Preheat your oven to 325°F (160°C). Grease a 9x5 inch (23x13 cm) loaf pan with vegetable oil and line the bottom with parchment paper.
2. In a mixing bowl, beat the eggs and sugar together using an electric mixer until pale and thickened. This may take about 8-10 minutes.
3. In a small saucepan, warm the milk, honey, and mirin over low heat until the honey is dissolved. Do not boil. Remove from heat and let it cool slightly.
4. Sift the cake flour and baking powder together into a separate bowl.
5. Gradually add the warm milk mixture to the beaten eggs, mixing continuously.
6. Gradually fold in the sifted flour mixture into the egg mixture until just combined. Be gentle to avoid deflating the batter.
7. Pour the batter into the prepared loaf pan and tap the pan gently on the counter to remove any air bubbles.
8. If desired, sprinkle sesame seeds over the top of the batter.
9. Bake in the preheated oven for about 50-60 minutes, or until the top is golden brown and a toothpick inserted into the center comes out clean.
10. Remove from the oven and let it cool in the pan for 10 minutes. Then, transfer it to a wire rack to cool completely.
11. Once cooled, slice and serve the Castella cake.

Castella can be stored in an airtight container at room temperature for a few days. Enjoy this delicious Japanese sponge cake with a cup of tea or coffee!

Ichigo Daifuku (Strawberry Mochi)

Ingredients:

- Fresh strawberries, washed and hulled
- Sweet red bean paste (anko)
- Mochiko (sweet rice flour)
- Granulated sugar
- Water
- Potato starch or cornstarch, for dusting

Instructions:

1. Prepare the sweet red bean paste (anko) or use store-bought if preferred.
2. Take a small amount of anko and flatten it into a disc in the palm of your hand.
3. Place a fresh strawberry on top of the anko disc and gently wrap the anko around the strawberry, covering it completely.
4. In a mixing bowl, combine mochiko (sweet rice flour) and granulated sugar. Gradually add water and mix until a smooth dough forms.
5. Transfer the dough to a microwave-safe dish and cover it with plastic wrap. Microwave on high for 1 minute.
6. Remove the dough from the microwave and knead it with a wet spatula. Re-cover with plastic wrap and microwave for another 30 seconds.
7. Remove the dough from the microwave and knead it again until smooth and elastic. If the dough is too dry, add a little water; if it's too wet, add a little more mochiko.
8. Dust a clean work surface with potato starch or cornstarch to prevent sticking. Take a small portion of the mochi dough and flatten it into a circle with your hands.
9. Place the anko-covered strawberry in the center of the mochi circle and wrap the mochi around the strawberry, sealing it completely.
10. Repeat the process with the remaining strawberries and mochi dough.
11. Serve the Ichigo Daifuku immediately, or store them in an airtight container in the refrigerator until ready to serve.

Ichigo Daifuku is best enjoyed fresh and chilled. The combination of the sweet red bean paste, fresh strawberry, and soft mochi creates a delightful harmony of flavors and textures. Enjoy this traditional Japanese sweet as a refreshing treat!

Warabi Mochi (Bracken Starch Dumplings)

Ingredients:

For the mochi:

- 100g warabi-ko (bracken starch)
- 2 cups (480ml) water
- 1/2 cup (100g) granulated sugar
- Kinako (roasted soybean flour), for dusting
- Kuromitsu (black sugar syrup), for serving

Instructions:

1. In a small bowl, mix the warabi-ko with 1 cup of water until smooth and well combined.
2. In a saucepan, bring the remaining 1 cup of water to a boil over medium heat. Once boiling, gradually add the warabi-ko mixture to the saucepan, stirring constantly to prevent lumps from forming.
3. Cook the mixture over medium heat, stirring constantly, until it thickens and becomes translucent, about 5-7 minutes.
4. Add the granulated sugar to the saucepan and continue to cook, stirring constantly, until the sugar is fully dissolved and the mixture thickens further, about 3-5 minutes.
5. Once the mixture has thickened, remove the saucepan from the heat and let it cool slightly.
6. While the mixture is still warm, pour it into a shallow dish or mold lined with plastic wrap to prevent sticking. Smooth out the surface with a spatula.
7. Let the warabi mochi cool to room temperature, then refrigerate for at least 1-2 hours, or until set firm.
8. Once set, remove the warabi mochi from the refrigerator and cut it into bite-sized pieces.
9. Dust the warabi mochi with kinako (roasted soybean flour) before serving.
10. Serve the warabi mochi with a drizzle of kuromitsu (black sugar syrup) on top.

Warabi mochi is best enjoyed chilled and has a unique chewy texture that's quite different from other types of mochi. It's a refreshing and delightful Japanese dessert, perfect for enjoying on a warm day!

Uiro (Steamed Rice Cake)

Ingredients:

- 200g rice flour (mochiko)
- 200g granulated sugar
- 400ml water
- 1 tablespoon matcha powder (optional, for green tea flavor)
- Kinako (roasted soybean flour) or katakuriko (potato starch), for dusting

Instructions:

1. In a mixing bowl, combine the rice flour and granulated sugar. If you're using matcha powder for green tea flavor, sift it into the bowl as well.
2. Gradually add water to the dry ingredients while stirring continuously to form a smooth batter. Make sure there are no lumps in the batter.
3. Transfer the batter to a saucepan and cook over medium heat, stirring constantly, until the mixture thickens and becomes translucent. This may take about 10-15 minutes.
4. Once the batter thickens, reduce the heat to low and continue to cook for another 5 minutes, stirring continuously to prevent burning.
5. While the batter is still hot, pour it into a square or rectangular mold lined with parchment paper. Smooth out the surface with a spatula.
6. Let the uiro batter cool to room temperature, then refrigerate for at least 1-2 hours, or until set firm.
7. Once set, remove the uiro from the mold and cut it into bite-sized pieces.
8. Dust the uiro pieces with kinako (roasted soybean flour) or katakuriko (potato starch) before serving to prevent sticking.
9. Serve the uiro as a sweet treat or dessert.

Uiro has a soft and slightly chewy texture with a delicate sweetness, making it a delightful Japanese snack or dessert. Enjoy its unique flavor and texture!

Matcha Cheesecake

Ingredients:

For the crust:

- 200g (about 7 oz) digestive biscuits or graham crackers
- 100g (about 7 tbsp) unsalted butter, melted

For the filling:

- 500g (about 2 cups) cream cheese, softened
- 150g (about 3/4 cup) granulated sugar
- 3 large eggs, at room temperature
- 1 tablespoon matcha powder
- 1 teaspoon vanilla extract
- 200ml (about 3/4 cup) heavy cream
- 1 tablespoon cornstarch

For the topping (optional):

- Whipped cream
- Matcha powder for dusting

Instructions:

1. Preheat your oven to 325°F (160°C). Grease a 9-inch (23cm) round springform pan and line the bottom with parchment paper.
2. Crush the digestive biscuits or graham crackers into fine crumbs. You can use a food processor or place them in a zip-top bag and crush them with a rolling pin. Mix the crumbs with melted butter until well combined.
3. Press the biscuit mixture into the bottom of the prepared springform pan, using the back of a spoon or your fingers to create an even layer. Refrigerate while you prepare the filling.
4. In a large mixing bowl, beat the cream cheese and granulated sugar together until smooth and creamy.

5. Add the eggs one at a time, beating well after each addition, until fully incorporated.
6. In a separate bowl, mix the matcha powder with a small amount of hot water to form a paste. Add this paste to the cream cheese mixture along with the vanilla extract and mix until evenly distributed.
7. In a small bowl, whisk together the heavy cream and cornstarch until smooth. Gradually add this mixture to the cream cheese mixture, beating until smooth and creamy.
8. Pour the cheesecake filling over the prepared crust in the springform pan, smoothing the top with a spatula.
9. Place the springform pan on a baking sheet to catch any drips and bake in the preheated oven for 45-50 minutes, or until the edges are set and the center is slightly jiggly.
10. Turn off the oven and leave the cheesecake inside with the door slightly ajar for about 1 hour to cool gradually.
11. Once cooled, refrigerate the cheesecake for at least 4 hours or overnight to set completely.
12. Before serving, carefully remove the cheesecake from the springform pan and transfer it to a serving plate. If desired, top with whipped cream and dust with matcha powder.
13. Slice and serve the matcha cheesecake chilled. Enjoy the creamy texture and subtle green tea flavor!

This matcha cheesecake is a delicious twist on a classic dessert, perfect for green tea lovers and special occasions.

Yatsuhashi (Cinnamon-flavored Rice Cake)

Ingredients:

For the dough:

- 200g (about 1 1/3 cups) joshinko (Japanese rice flour)
- 100g (about 1/2 cup) granulated sugar
- 120ml (about 1/2 cup) water
- 1 teaspoon ground cinnamon
- 1 tablespoon kinako (roasted soybean flour), for dusting

For the filling (optional):

- 150g (about 5 oz) sweet red bean paste (anko)

Instructions:

1. In a mixing bowl, combine the joshinko (Japanese rice flour), granulated sugar, ground cinnamon, and water. Stir until the mixture comes together into a dough.
2. Transfer the dough to a clean work surface dusted with joshinko or potato starch to prevent sticking. Knead the dough until smooth and elastic.
3. Roll out the dough into a thin sheet, about 1/8 inch (3mm) thick.
4. Using a knife or pizza cutter, cut the dough into rectangular shapes, about 3 inches (7.5cm) long and 2 inches (5cm) wide.
5. If you're adding filling, place a small amount of sweet red bean paste (anko) onto one half of each dough rectangle.
6. Fold the dough over the filling to form a triangle, pressing the edges to seal.
7. Heat a non-stick pan over medium heat. Place the filled yatsuhashi triangles in the pan and cook for 1-2 minutes on each side, until lightly golden brown and cooked through.
8. Remove the cooked yatsuhashi from the pan and let them cool slightly.
9. Dust the yatsuhashi with kinako (roasted soybean flour) before serving.
10. Enjoy the yatsuhashi as a delicious sweet treat!

Yatsuhashi is typically enjoyed as is, but you can also experiment with different fillings such as chocolate, fruit jam, or even Nutella for a modern twist.

Hanami Dango (Tri-colored Dumplings)

Ingredients:

For the dango:

- 200g (about 1 1/3 cups) shiratamako (sweet rice flour)
- 60ml (about 1/4 cup) water
- 1-2 drops red food coloring
- 1-2 drops green food coloring
- 1-2 drops yellow food coloring

For the sweet soy glaze:

- 3 tablespoons soy sauce
- 3 tablespoons mirin (Japanese sweet rice wine)
- 3 tablespoons granulated sugar

Instructions:

1. In a mixing bowl, combine the shiratamako (sweet rice flour) with water. Mix until it forms a smooth, pliable dough. If the dough is too dry, add a little more water; if it's too wet, add a little more shiratamako.
2. Divide the dough into three equal portions.
3. Add a drop or two of red food coloring to one portion of the dough and knead until the color is evenly distributed, forming a pink dough. Repeat with green food coloring for another portion and yellow food coloring for the last portion.
4. Take small pieces of each colored dough and roll them into small balls, about 1 inch (2.5cm) in diameter.
5. Bring a pot of water to a boil. Drop the dango balls into the boiling water and cook until they float to the surface, about 2-3 minutes.
6. Remove the cooked dango from the pot and immediately plunge them into a bowl of cold water to stop the cooking process. Drain well.
7. Thread the dango balls onto skewers, alternating the colors to create a tri-colored pattern.

8. In a small saucepan, combine the soy sauce, mirin, and granulated sugar for the sweet soy glaze. Heat over medium heat, stirring constantly, until the sugar is dissolved and the mixture thickens slightly.
9. Brush the sweet soy glaze over the dango skewers.
10. Serve the Hanami Dango as a delightful and colorful sweet treat, perfect for hanami picnics or any springtime celebration!

Hanami Dango is not only visually appealing but also has a chewy texture and a subtle sweetness that makes it a delightful traditional Japanese dessert. Enjoy it with friends and family under the cherry blossoms!

Kintsuba (Sweet Bean Paste Cake)

Ingredients:

For the dough:

- 200g (about 1 1/3 cups) all-purpose flour
- 100ml (about 1/2 cup) water

For the sweet bean paste filling:

- 200g (about 1 cup) sweet red bean paste (anko)

For the glaze:

- 2 tablespoons granulated sugar
- 2 tablespoons water

Instructions:

1. In a mixing bowl, combine the all-purpose flour and water to form a smooth dough. Knead the dough until it becomes elastic and pliable. If the dough is too dry, add a little more water; if it's too wet, add a little more flour.
2. Divide the dough into equal portions and roll each portion into a ball. Flatten each ball into a thin disk, about 1/8 inch (3mm) thick.
3. Place a spoonful of sweet red bean paste (anko) onto the center of each dough disk.
4. Fold the edges of the dough over the bean paste to enclose it completely, forming a square or rectangular shape. Press the edges firmly to seal.
5. Preheat a non-stick pan or griddle over medium heat. Lightly grease the surface with oil or butter.
6. Place the filled dough squares onto the pan and cook for 2-3 minutes on each side, or until lightly golden brown and cooked through.
7. In a small saucepan, combine the granulated sugar and water for the glaze. Heat over medium heat, stirring constantly, until the sugar is dissolved and the mixture thickens slightly.

8. Brush the sweet bean paste cakes (kintsuba) with the sugar glaze while they are still warm.
9. Serve the kintsuba as a delicious and traditional Japanese sweet.

Kintsuba has a delicate balance of sweetness from the red bean paste and a slightly crispy texture from the grilled dough. Enjoy this delightful treat with a cup of green tea for a taste of Japanese confectionery tradition!

Kinako Mochi (Roasted Soybean Flour Rice Cake)

Ingredients:

For the mochi:

- 1 cup (200g) mochiko (sweet rice flour)
- 1 cup (240ml) water
- 1/4 cup (50g) granulated sugar
- Potato starch or cornstarch, for dusting

For the coating:

- 1/2 cup (50g) kinako (roasted soybean flour)
- 2-3 tablespoons granulated sugar (optional, adjust to taste)

For the syrup (optional):

- 2 tablespoons kuromitsu (black sugar syrup)
- 1 tablespoon water

Instructions:

1. In a microwave-safe bowl, mix together the mochiko, water, and granulated sugar until well combined.
2. Cover the bowl loosely with plastic wrap and microwave on high for 2 minutes.
3. Carefully remove the bowl from the microwave and stir the mixture with a wet spatula. It will be very sticky.
4. Re-cover the bowl and microwave for another 1-2 minutes, or until the mixture is cooked and translucent.
5. Dust a clean work surface with potato starch or cornstarch to prevent sticking. Transfer the cooked mochi dough onto the dusted surface.
6. While the mochi is still warm, divide it into equal portions and roll each portion into a ball or square shape.
7. In a separate bowl, mix together the kinako and granulated sugar for the coating.
8. Roll each mochi ball or square in the kinako mixture until evenly coated.

9. If desired, prepare the syrup by mixing the kuromitsu with water in a small saucepan and heating it over low heat until warmed.
10. Serve the kinako mochi immediately, drizzled with the syrup if using.

Kinako mochi is best enjoyed fresh, as the mochi tends to harden over time. The combination of the chewy mochi and nutty kinako creates a delightful contrast of textures and flavors. Enjoy this traditional Japanese sweet as a snack or dessert!

Sakura Anpan (Cherry Blossom Sweet Bun)

Ingredients:

For the dough:

- 300g (about 2 cups) all-purpose flour
- 50g (about 1/4 cup) granulated sugar
- 1 teaspoon active dry yeast
- 150ml (about 2/3 cup) warm milk
- 30g (about 2 tablespoons) unsalted butter, melted
- 1 egg
- Pinch of salt

For the filling:

- 200g (about 1 cup) sweet red bean paste (anko)

For the cherry blossom decoration:

- A small amount of dough reserved from the main dough
- Pink food coloring (optional)

Instructions:

1. In a mixing bowl, combine the warm milk, granulated sugar, and active dry yeast. Let it sit for about 5-10 minutes, or until foamy.
2. Add the flour, melted butter, egg, and salt to the yeast mixture. Mix until a dough forms.
3. Knead the dough on a lightly floured surface until smooth and elastic. Place the dough in a greased bowl, cover with a clean towel or plastic wrap, and let it rise in a warm place for about 1 hour, or until doubled in size.
4. Once the dough has risen, punch it down and divide it into equal portions, depending on how many buns you want to make.
5. Take each portion of dough and flatten it into a small circle. Place a spoonful of sweet red bean paste (anko) in the center of each circle.

6. Gather the edges of the dough and pinch them together to enclose the filling, forming a smooth ball. Place the balls seam side down on a baking sheet lined with parchment paper.
7. To make the cherry blossom decoration, take a small amount of reserved dough and knead in a drop of pink food coloring until evenly colored. Roll out the pink dough and cut it into small pieces to form the petals of the cherry blossom.
8. Gently press the cherry blossom petals onto the top of each bun.
9. Let the buns rise for another 30-45 minutes, or until slightly puffed.
10. Preheat your oven to 350°F (180°C). Bake the buns for 15-20 minutes, or until golden brown.
11. Remove the buns from the oven and let them cool on a wire rack before serving.
12. Enjoy the Sakura Anpan as a delightful and beautiful Japanese sweet treat!

These Sakura Anpan buns are not only delicious but also visually appealing, making them perfect for special occasions or as a charming addition to your afternoon tea.

Sata Andagi (Okinawan Doughnuts)

Ingredients:

- 2 cups (250g) all-purpose flour
- 1/2 cup (100g) granulated sugar
- 2 large eggs
- 1 teaspoon baking powder
- 1/4 cup (60ml) whole milk
- 1 teaspoon vanilla extract (optional)
- Vegetable oil, for frying

Instructions:

1. In a large mixing bowl, whisk together the eggs and granulated sugar until well combined.
2. Add the flour, baking powder, whole milk, and vanilla extract (if using) to the egg mixture. Stir until a smooth batter forms.
3. Heat vegetable oil in a deep fryer or heavy-bottomed pot to 350°F (180°C).
4. Using a spoon or cookie scoop, drop spoonfuls of batter into the hot oil, being careful not to overcrowd the pot.
5. Fry the doughnut holes for 3-4 minutes, or until they are golden brown and cooked through, flipping them halfway through cooking.
6. Remove the fried doughnuts from the oil using a slotted spoon and drain them on paper towels to remove excess oil.
7. Allow the Sata Andagi to cool slightly before serving.
8. Enjoy the Sata Andagi as a delicious and nostalgic Okinawan treat!

These Sata Andagi doughnuts are crispy on the outside and fluffy on the inside, with a delightful sweetness that makes them irresistible. They are perfect for snacking or enjoying with a cup of tea or coffee.

Karukan (Sweet Potato Cake)

Ingredients:

- 200g (about 1 1/2 cups) sweet potato flour (satsumaimo-ko)
- 100g (about 1/2 cup) granulated sugar
- 150ml (about 2/3 cup) water
- Katakuriko (potato starch) or cornstarch, for dusting

Instructions:

1. In a mixing bowl, combine the sweet potato flour and granulated sugar.
2. Gradually add water to the dry ingredients while stirring continuously to form a smooth batter.
3. Preheat your steamer over medium heat.
4. Line a steaming tray or dish with parchment paper and lightly grease it with oil.
5. Pour the batter into the prepared steaming tray, spreading it out evenly with a spatula.
6. Place the steaming tray into the preheated steamer and steam the batter for about 20-25 minutes, or until set and cooked through.
7. Once cooked, remove the steaming tray from the steamer and let the karukan cool to room temperature.
8. Dust a clean work surface with katakuriko or cornstarch to prevent sticking. Transfer the cooled karukan onto the dusted surface.
9. Using a knife or cookie cutter, cut the karukan into desired shapes, such as squares or rectangles.
10. Dust the cut karukan pieces with katakuriko or cornstarch to prevent them from sticking together.
11. Serve the karukan as a delicious and traditional Japanese sweet.

Karukan has a soft and chewy texture with a delicate sweetness, making it a delightful treat to enjoy with tea or coffee. Store any leftover karukan in an airtight container at room temperature for up to several days. Enjoy!

Mitarashi Kushi Dango (Skewered Rice Dumplings with Sweet Soy Sauce)

Ingredients:

For the dango:

- 1 cup (200g) mochiko (sweet rice flour)
- 1/2 cup (120ml) water
- Optional: food coloring (such as matcha powder for green color)

For the sweet soy sauce glaze (mitarashi):

- 1/4 cup (60ml) soy sauce
- 1/4 cup (60ml) water
- 2 tablespoons granulated sugar
- 1 tablespoon potato starch or cornstarch
- 1 tablespoon mirin (Japanese sweet rice wine)

For skewering:

- Bamboo skewers

Instructions:

1. In a mixing bowl, combine the mochiko and water. Mix until a smooth dough forms. If desired, add a small amount of food coloring to the dough for color variation.
2. Divide the dough into equal portions and roll each portion into small balls, about 1 inch (2.5cm) in diameter.
3. Bring a pot of water to a boil. Drop the dango balls into the boiling water and cook until they float to the surface, about 2-3 minutes.
4. Remove the cooked dango from the pot and immediately plunge them into a bowl of cold water to stop the cooking process. Drain well.
5. Thread the cooked dango balls onto bamboo skewers, dividing them evenly among the skewers.

6. In a saucepan, combine the soy sauce, water, granulated sugar, mirin, and potato starch or cornstarch for the sweet soy sauce glaze. Stir until the sugar is dissolved and the starch is well incorporated.
7. Place the saucepan over medium heat and bring the mixture to a simmer. Cook, stirring constantly, until the sauce thickens to a glaze consistency, about 2-3 minutes.
8. Brush the sweet soy sauce glaze generously over the skewered dango, coating them evenly.
9. Grill the skewered dango over medium heat or broil them in the oven until lightly charred and caramelized, about 2-3 minutes per side.
10. Serve the Mitarashi Kushi Dango immediately, either as is or with extra glaze drizzled on top.

Mitarashi Kushi Dango is a delicious and popular Japanese sweet, perfect for snacking or enjoying as a dessert. The combination of chewy dango and sweet-savory soy sauce glaze creates a delightful harmony of flavors and textures. Enjoy!

Kuri Kinton (Candied Sweet Potatoes with Chestnuts)

Ingredients:

- 500g (about 1 lb) sweet potatoes
- 200g (about 7 oz) cooked and peeled chestnuts
- 200g (about 1 cup) granulated sugar
- 100ml (about 1/2 cup) water
- Pinch of salt
- Kinako (roasted soybean flour) or sesame seeds, for garnish (optional)

Instructions:

1. Peel the sweet potatoes and cut them into chunks or slices. Rinse them in cold water to remove excess starch.
2. In a large pot, combine the sweet potatoes, cooked chestnuts, sugar, water, and a pinch of salt.
3. Bring the mixture to a boil over medium heat, then reduce the heat to low and simmer gently, stirring occasionally, until the sweet potatoes are tender and the liquid has thickened to a syrupy consistency. This may take about 20-30 minutes.
4. Mash the sweet potatoes and chestnuts with a potato masher or the back of a spoon until smooth and creamy. Be careful not to overmash, as you still want some texture.
5. Continue to cook the mixture over low heat, stirring constantly, until it thickens further and becomes glossy, about 10-15 minutes.
6. Remove the pot from the heat and let the kuri kinton cool slightly.
7. Once cooled, shape the kuri kinton into small balls or mound-shaped portions using a spoon or your hands.
8. If desired, roll the kuri kinton in kinako (roasted soybean flour) or sesame seeds for added flavor and texture.
9. Serve the kuri kinton as a sweet and festive treat, especially during autumn and winter seasons.

Kuri kinton is a delightful Japanese sweet with a rich and creamy texture, perfect for celebrating special occasions or enjoying as a comforting dessert.

Momiji Manju (Maple Leaf-shaped Cake with Sweet Bean Paste)

Ingredients:

For the dough:

- 100g (about 3/4 cup) cake flour
- 1/2 teaspoon baking powder
- 2 tablespoons granulated sugar
- 1 egg
- 2 tablespoons milk
- 1 tablespoon vegetable oil

For the filling:

- 200g (about 1 cup) sweet red bean paste (anko)

Instructions:

1. Preheat your oven to 350°F (180°C). Grease a maple leaf-shaped mold or muffin tin with vegetable oil.
2. In a mixing bowl, sift together the cake flour and baking powder. Add the granulated sugar and mix well.
3. In a separate bowl, beat the egg lightly, then add the milk and vegetable oil. Mix until well combined.
4. Gradually add the wet ingredients to the dry ingredients, stirring until you have a smooth batter.
5. Fill each cavity of the maple leaf-shaped mold or muffin tin with a thin layer of batter, about halfway full.
6. Spoon a small amount of sweet red bean paste (anko) onto the center of each batter-filled cavity.
7. Cover the red bean paste with more batter until the cavity is about 3/4 full.
8. Smooth the surface of the batter with a spatula.
9. Bake in the preheated oven for about 15-20 minutes, or until the Momiji Manju are golden brown and a toothpick inserted into the center comes out clean.
10. Remove the Momiji Manju from the oven and let them cool in the mold or muffin tin for a few minutes.

11. Carefully remove the Momiji Manju from the mold or muffin tin and transfer them to a wire rack to cool completely.
12. Serve the Momiji Manju as a delightful and traditional Japanese sweet.

Momiji Manju is best enjoyed fresh, but you can store any leftovers in an airtight container at room temperature for up to a few days. Enjoy the sweet bean paste-filled treats with a cup of tea or coffee for a delightful snack or dessert!

Amazake (Sweet Fermented Rice Drink)

Ingredients:

- 1 cup (200g) short-grain white rice
- 2 cups (480ml) water
- 1/4 cup (50g) koji rice (also known as koji-kin or rice koji)

Instructions:

1. Rinse the rice under cold water until the water runs clear.
2. In a large bowl, combine the rinsed rice and water. Let the rice soak for at least 6 hours or overnight.
3. After soaking, drain the rice and transfer it to a rice cooker. Add fresh water to cover the rice, then cook the rice according to the rice cooker instructions.
4. Once the rice is cooked, transfer it to a large bowl and let it cool to about 140°F (60°C). This is the ideal temperature for fermenting with koji.
5. Add the koji rice to the cooked rice and mix well to combine.
6. Cover the bowl with a clean kitchen towel or plastic wrap and let it ferment in a warm place (around 120°F or 50°C) for about 8-12 hours. You can use a yogurt maker, a dehydrator set to low, or simply place the bowl in a warm spot in your kitchen.
7. After the fermentation period, the mixture should have a slightly sweet and tangy flavor. It will thicken slightly as it cools.
8. Once cooled to room temperature, transfer the amazake to a clean, airtight container and store it in the refrigerator. It will keep for about 3-4 days.
9. Serve the amazake chilled or warmed, depending on your preference. You can also blend it with a bit of water or milk to make it smoother.
10. Enjoy the homemade amazake as a nutritious and delicious drink!

Amazake is not only tasty but also packed with nutrients and probiotics, making it a great choice for a healthy beverage. You can also use it as a natural sweetener in various recipes or enjoy it as a dessert on its own.

Kasutera (Japanese Honey Castella Cake)

Ingredients:

- 4 large eggs
- 120g (about 1/2 cup) granulated sugar
- 80g (about 1/4 cup) honey
- 1 tablespoon mirin (Japanese sweet rice wine) or white wine (optional)
- 100g (about 3/4 cup) cake flour
- 1/2 teaspoon baking powder
- Vegetable oil or butter, for greasing the pan

Instructions:

1. Preheat your oven to 320°F (160°C). Grease a loaf pan with vegetable oil or butter and line it with parchment paper, leaving some overhang on the sides for easy removal.
2. In a heatproof bowl, whisk together the eggs and granulated sugar.
3. Place the bowl over a pot of simmering water (double boiler) and continue whisking until the mixture becomes warm to the touch and the sugar has dissolved. Be careful not to let the bottom of the bowl touch the water.
4. Remove the bowl from the heat and continue whisking until the mixture becomes pale and thick, and leaves a ribbon trail when you lift the whisk. This may take about 5-7 minutes.
5. Warm the honey in the microwave or over low heat until it becomes more fluid. Add the warm honey and mirin (if using) to the egg mixture and whisk until well combined.
6. Sift the cake flour and baking powder into the egg mixture and gently fold until just combined. Be careful not to overmix, as this can deflate the batter.
7. Pour the batter into the prepared loaf pan and tap the pan gently on the countertop to remove any air bubbles.
8. Bake in the preheated oven for about 40-50 minutes, or until the top is golden brown and a toothpick inserted into the center comes out clean.
9. Remove the cake from the oven and let it cool in the pan for about 10 minutes. Then, transfer it to a wire rack to cool completely.
10. Once cooled, slice the Kasutera into pieces and serve. Enjoy the delicious Japanese Honey Castella Cake with a cup of tea or coffee!

Kasutera is a beloved Japanese dessert with a delicate texture and a sweet, fragrant flavor from the honey. It's perfect for special occasions or as a delightful treat any time of the day.

Senbei (Rice Crackers)

Ingredients:

- 1 cup (200g) short-grain Japanese rice (such as sushi rice)
- 1 1/2 cups (360ml) water
- Soy sauce or other seasonings of your choice (e.g., salt, sugar, sesame seeds, seaweed, etc.)
- Vegetable oil for brushing

Instructions:

1. Rinse the rice under cold water until the water runs clear. Drain well.
2. In a rice cooker or pot, combine the rinsed rice and water. Cook the rice according to the rice cooker instructions or until it's fully cooked and slightly sticky.
3. Transfer the cooked rice to a large bowl and let it cool slightly.
4. Preheat your oven to 350°F (180°C). Line a baking sheet with parchment paper.
5. Once the rice has cooled down enough to handle, divide it into small portions. The size and thickness of the senbei are up to you, but keep in mind that thinner senbei will be crispier.
6. Place a portion of the cooked rice between two sheets of plastic wrap or parchment paper. Flatten the rice into a thin, even layer using a rolling pin or your hands. Aim for about 1/8 to 1/4 inch (3 to 6mm) thickness.
7. Carefully peel off the top layer of plastic wrap or parchment paper. Use a cookie cutter or knife to cut the flattened rice into desired shapes, such as circles or squares.
8. Transfer the cut rice crackers onto the prepared baking sheet. Leave some space between each cracker.
9. Brush the top of each rice cracker with a thin layer of soy sauce or other seasonings of your choice, such as salt, sugar, sesame seeds, or crushed seaweed.
10. Bake the senbei in the preheated oven for about 20-25 minutes, or until they are crisp and golden brown around the edges. Keep an eye on them as they can burn quickly.
11. Remove the senbei from the oven and let them cool completely on the baking sheet.
12. Once cooled, store the senbei in an airtight container at room temperature. They should stay crisp for several days.

Enjoy your homemade senbei as a crunchy and flavorful snack! Experiment with different seasonings and shapes to create your own unique variations.

Kuri Mochi (Chestnut Rice Cake)

Ingredients:

- 200g (about 1 1/4 cups) mochiko (glutinous rice flour)
- 200g (about 7 oz) cooked and peeled chestnuts, mashed or finely chopped
- 100g (about 1/2 cup) granulated sugar
- 200ml (about 3/4 cup plus 2 tablespoons) water
- Potato starch or cornstarch, for dusting

Instructions:

1. In a mixing bowl, combine the mochiko, mashed or chopped chestnuts, granulated sugar, and water. Mix until well combined into a smooth batter.
2. Transfer the mixture to a heatproof dish or bowl suitable for steaming.
3. Place the dish in a steamer basket over boiling water, cover, and steam for about 30-40 minutes, or until the mochi is cooked through and has a slightly translucent appearance.
4. Once the mochi is cooked, remove it from the steamer and let it cool slightly.
5. Dust a clean work surface with potato starch or cornstarch to prevent sticking. Transfer the warm mochi onto the dusted surface.
6. Divide the mochi into equal portions and shape each portion into a ball or disk.
7. Serve the Kuri Mochi immediately, or let it cool completely before serving.

Kuri Mochi is a delicious and chewy Japanese sweet with a subtle chestnut flavor. Enjoy it as a snack or dessert with a cup of tea or alongside other traditional Japanese sweets. Store any leftovers in an airtight container at room temperature for up to several days.

Shiratama Dango (Rice Dumplings)

Ingredients:

- 1 cup (150g) shiratamako (glutinous rice flour)
- 1/2 cup (120ml) water
- Additional cornstarch or potato starch for dusting

Instructions:

1. In a mixing bowl, combine the shiratamako and water. Mix well until a smooth dough forms. If the dough is too dry, add a little more water, a teaspoon at a time, until the dough comes together.
2. Divide the dough into small portions and roll each portion into a ball, about 1 inch (2.5 cm) in diameter.
3. Bring a pot of water to a boil over medium heat. Drop the shiratama dango into the boiling water, stirring gently to prevent sticking.
4. Cook the dango for about 2-3 minutes, or until they float to the surface and are translucent.
5. Use a slotted spoon to transfer the cooked dango to a bowl of cold water to stop the cooking process.
6. Once cooled, remove the dango from the water and drain them well.
7. Dust a clean work surface with cornstarch or potato starch to prevent sticking. Transfer the drained dango onto the dusted surface.
8. Serve the shiratama dango with sweet red bean paste (anko), syrup, or your favorite toppings.

Shiratama dango can be enjoyed in various traditional Japanese desserts such as Shiratama Anmitsu, Shiratama Zenzai, or Shiratama Mitarashi Dango. They add a delightful chewy texture to any sweet dish and are easy to make at home. Enjoy experimenting with different toppings and flavors!

Hishi Mochi (Diamond-shaped Rice Cakes)

Ingredients:

For the mochi:

- 1 cup (150g) mochiko (glutinous rice flour)
- 1/4 cup (50g) granulated sugar
- 3/4 cup (180ml) water
- Food coloring (pink, white, and green)

For dusting:

- Potato starch or cornstarch

Instructions:

1. In a microwave-safe bowl, combine the mochiko and granulated sugar. Mix well.
2. Gradually add water to the mochiko mixture, stirring until smooth and well combined.
3. Divide the mochi mixture into three equal portions.
4. Add a few drops of pink food coloring to one portion of the mochi mixture and mix until evenly colored.
5. Leave one portion of the mochi mixture uncolored (white).
6. Add a few drops of green food coloring to the remaining portion of the mochi mixture and mix until evenly colored.
7. Place each portion of colored mochi mixture into a separate microwave-safe dish.
8. Microwave each dish of mochi mixture separately on high for 1-2 minutes, or until the mochi is cooked and becomes translucent. The cooking time may vary depending on your microwave, so keep an eye on it.
9. Dust a clean work surface with potato starch or cornstarch to prevent sticking.
10. While the mochi is still warm, divide each color into four equal portions and roll each portion into a ball.
11. Flatten each mochi ball into a thin, oval-shaped disk.
12. Arrange one pink, one white, and one green mochi disk on top of each other, slightly overlapping, to form a diamond shape.

13. Press the layers together gently to adhere.
14. Repeat the process with the remaining mochi portions to make more Hishi Mochi.
15. Serve the Hishi Mochi as a traditional Japanese treat for Hinamatsuri or other special occasions.

Hishi Mochi is not only delicious but also visually appealing with its vibrant colors and unique diamond shape. Enjoy this special Japanese sweet with your family and friends!

Mizu Yokan (Water Yokan)

Ingredients:

- 20g (about 2 tablespoons) kanten (agar agar) powder or agar agar flakes
- 800ml (about 3 1/3 cups) water
- 200g (about 1 cup) granulated sugar
- 200g (about 1 cup) sweet red bean paste (anko)

Instructions:

1. In a saucepan, combine the water and kanten (agar agar) powder or flakes. Let it soak for about 10-15 minutes.
2. After soaking, heat the mixture over medium heat, stirring constantly, until the agar agar is completely dissolved.
3. Add the granulated sugar to the saucepan and continue to stir until the sugar is completely dissolved.
4. Remove the saucepan from the heat and let the mixture cool slightly.
5. Meanwhile, prepare a rectangular or square mold by lining it with plastic wrap or parchment paper.
6. Once the mixture has cooled down a bit, pour a thin layer of the agar agar mixture into the bottom of the mold.
7. Place the mold in the refrigerator and let the agar agar layer set for about 15-20 minutes, or until it becomes slightly firm.
8. Remove the mold from the refrigerator and spread a layer of sweet red bean paste (anko) evenly over the partially set agar agar layer.
9. Pour the remaining agar agar mixture over the red bean paste layer, covering it completely.
10. Return the mold to the refrigerator and let the Mizu Yokan set completely, preferably for several hours or overnight.
11. Once set, remove the Mizu Yokan from the mold by lifting the plastic wrap or parchment paper.
12. Slice the Mizu Yokan into individual servings and serve chilled.

Mizu Yokan is a delightful and refreshing Japanese dessert, perfect for enjoying on hot summer days or as a sweet ending to any meal. Feel free to experiment with different flavors of anko or add fruits for variation. Enjoy!

Yubeshi (Citrus-flavored Rice Cake)

Ingredients:

- 200g (about 1 1/4 cups) mochiko (glutinous rice flour)
- 100g (about 1/2 cup) granulated sugar
- 100ml (about 1/2 cup) water
- 50g (about 1/4 cup) sweet red bean paste (anko)
- 1 yuzu (or substitute with lemon or orange zest)
- Additional granulated sugar for coating (optional)

Instructions:

1. In a mixing bowl, combine the mochiko, granulated sugar, and water. Mix until well combined into a smooth dough.
2. Divide the dough into small portions, each about the size of a ping pong ball.
3. Flatten each portion of dough into a small disk, about 1/4 inch (6mm) thick.
4. Place a small amount of sweet red bean paste (anko) in the center of each dough disk.
5. Fold the edges of the dough over the red bean paste to enclose it completely, shaping it into a small ball or oval.
6. Grate the zest of the yuzu (or lemon/orange) and sprinkle it over the surface of the Yubeshi.
7. Optionally, roll each Yubeshi in granulated sugar to coat the outside.
8. Place the Yubeshi on a baking sheet lined with parchment paper and bake in a preheated oven at 350°F (180°C) for about 15-20 minutes, or until they are slightly golden brown on the outside.
9. Remove the Yubeshi from the oven and let them cool completely before serving.

Yubeshi is a delightful Japanese sweet with a unique citrus flavor and a chewy texture from the mochiko. Enjoy it as a snack or dessert with a cup of tea, or share it with friends and family during special occasions.

Kuri Anmitsu (Chestnut Jelly Dessert)

Ingredients:

For the agar agar jelly:

- 10g (about 2 teaspoons) agar agar powder or flakes
- 800ml (about 3 1/3 cups) water
- 100g (about 1/2 cup) granulated sugar

For the sweet red bean paste (anko):

- 200g (about 1 cup) cooked and sweetened red beans (azuki beans)
- 2-3 tablespoons granulated sugar (adjust to taste)

For serving:

- Boiled chestnuts (kuri)
- Fresh fruit slices (such as strawberries, kiwi, or mandarin oranges)
- Shiratama dango (small rice dumplings, optional)
- Kuromitsu (brown sugar syrup) or honey, for drizzling
- Toasted sesame seeds, for garnish

Instructions:

1. Start by preparing the agar agar jelly. In a saucepan, combine the agar agar powder or flakes with water. Let it soak for about 10 minutes.
2. After soaking, heat the mixture over medium heat, stirring constantly, until the agar agar is completely dissolved.
3. Add the granulated sugar to the saucepan and continue to stir until the sugar is completely dissolved.
4. Remove the saucepan from the heat and let the mixture cool slightly. Then, pour it into a shallow dish or mold. Let it set in the refrigerator for about 1-2 hours, or until firm.
5. Meanwhile, prepare the sweet red bean paste (anko). In a saucepan, combine the cooked and sweetened red beans with granulated sugar. Cook over low heat,

stirring constantly, until the mixture thickens to a paste-like consistency. Remove from heat and let it cool.
6. Once the agar agar jelly has set, cut it into cubes or small rectangles.
7. To serve, place a few pieces of agar agar jelly in a bowl or dish. Add a spoonful of sweet red bean paste (anko) on top.
8. Arrange boiled chestnuts (kuri) and fresh fruit slices around the jelly and red bean paste.
9. If using, add shiratama dango (small rice dumplings) to the bowl.
10. Drizzle kuromitsu (brown sugar syrup) or honey over the dessert.
11. Garnish with toasted sesame seeds for added flavor and texture.
12. Serve the Kuri Anmitsu chilled and enjoy!

Kuri Anmitsu is a delightful and refreshing Japanese dessert, perfect for enjoying during warmer months or as a sweet treat any time of the year. Feel free to customize it with your favorite toppings and flavors.

Kuzumanju (Steamed Wheat Cake)

Ingredients:

- 60g (about 1/2 cup) kuzuko (kudzu starch)
- 2 tablespoons granulated sugar
- 300ml (about 1 1/4 cups) water
- Kuromitsu (black sugar syrup), for serving
- Kinako (roasted soybean flour), for serving

Instructions:

1. In a small saucepan, combine the kuzuko (kudzu starch) and granulated sugar. Mix well to combine.
2. Gradually add the water to the saucepan, stirring continuously to prevent lumps from forming.
3. Place the saucepan over medium heat and cook the mixture, stirring constantly, until it thickens and becomes translucent. This should take about 5-7 minutes.
4. Once the mixture has thickened, remove the saucepan from the heat and let it cool slightly.
5. While the mixture is still warm, pour it into small molds or a shallow dish lined with plastic wrap.
6. Let the kuzumochi cool and set at room temperature for about 30 minutes to 1 hour, or until firm.
7. Once the kuzumochi is set, remove it from the molds or dish and cut it into bite-sized pieces.
8. To serve, drizzle kuromitsu (black sugar syrup) over the kuzumochi and sprinkle with kinako (roasted soybean flour).
9. Enjoy the kuzumochi as a delicious and refreshing Japanese sweet treat!

Kuzumochi is a delightful dessert with a unique texture and flavor. It's perfect for enjoying on its own or as a sweet ending to a Japanese meal. Adjust the sweetness according to your taste preferences and feel free to experiment with different toppings or variations.

Goma Dango (Sesame Dumplings)

Ingredients:

For the dumplings:

- 1 cup (150g) shiratamako (glutinous rice flour)
- 2 tablespoons black sesame seeds
- 2 tablespoons granulated sugar
- About 1/2 cup (120ml) warm water

For the coating:

- Additional black sesame seeds, toasted and finely ground
- Granulated sugar (optional)

Instructions:

1. In a dry skillet, toast the black sesame seeds over medium heat until fragrant, about 2-3 minutes. Be careful not to burn them. Let the sesame seeds cool.
2. Grind the toasted sesame seeds in a food processor or mortar and pestle until finely ground. Set aside.
3. In a mixing bowl, combine the shiratamako, ground sesame seeds, and granulated sugar. Mix well.
4. Gradually add warm water to the dry ingredients, stirring constantly, until a smooth dough forms. You may need slightly more or less water depending on the humidity and moisture content of the flour.
5. Once the dough comes together, divide it into small portions and roll each portion into a ball, about 1 inch (2.5 cm) in diameter.
6. Bring a pot of water to a boil over medium heat. Drop the dumplings into the boiling water, stirring gently to prevent sticking.
7. Cook the dumplings for about 2-3 minutes, or until they float to the surface and are slightly translucent.
8. Use a slotted spoon to transfer the cooked dumplings to a bowl of cold water to stop the cooking process.
9. Once cooled, remove the dumplings from the water and drain them well.
10. Roll the drained dumplings in the ground sesame seeds until evenly coated.

11. Optionally, sprinkle the coated dumplings with granulated sugar for added sweetness.
12. Serve the Goma Dango as a delightful Japanese sweet treat!

Goma Dango is best enjoyed fresh, but you can also store any leftovers in an airtight container in the refrigerator for up to a few days. Enjoy the chewy and nutty flavor of these delicious sesame dumplings with a cup of green tea or as a sweet snack anytime.

Yomogi Mochi (Japanese Mugwort Rice Cake)

Ingredients:

- 200g (about 1 1/4 cups) mochiko (glutinous rice flour)
- 100g (about 1/2 cup) granulated sugar
- 200ml (about 3/4 cup plus 2 tablespoons) water
- 100g (about 3.5 oz) fresh yomogi leaves (Japanese mugwort leaves), washed and finely chopped
- Potato starch or cornstarch, for dusting

Instructions:

1. In a mixing bowl, combine the mochiko and granulated sugar. Mix well.
2. In a blender or food processor, blend the chopped yomogi leaves with water until smooth.
3. Strain the yomogi mixture through a fine-mesh sieve to remove any solid bits. You should have about 200ml of yomogi liquid.
4. Gradually add the yomogi liquid to the mochiko mixture, stirring continuously to form a smooth batter.
5. Transfer the batter to a heatproof dish or bowl suitable for steaming.
6. Steam the batter over boiling water for about 30-40 minutes, or until it's cooked through and becomes slightly translucent.
7. Once cooked, remove the dish from the steamer and let the mochi cool slightly.
8. Dust a clean work surface with potato starch or cornstarch to prevent sticking.
9. Transfer the warm mochi onto the dusted surface.
10. Divide the mochi into equal portions and shape each portion into a ball or disk.
11. Serve the Yomogi Mochi immediately, or let it cool completely before serving.

Yomogi Mochi is a delightful Japanese sweet with a unique green color and earthy flavor from the yomogi leaves. Enjoy it as a snack or dessert with a cup of green tea, or alongside other traditional Japanese sweets. Store any leftovers in an airtight container at room temperature for up to several days.

Hanabiramochi (Cherry Blossom Rice Cake)

Ingredients:

For the mochi:

- 1 cup (150g) mochiko (glutinous rice flour)
- 1/4 cup (50g) granulated sugar
- 3/4 cup (180ml) water
- Potato starch or cornstarch, for dusting

For the filling:

- 200g (about 1 cup) sweet red bean paste (anko)

For decoration:

- Pickled cherry blossom leaves (sakura leaves), rinsed and patted dry
- Edible gold or silver leaf (optional, for decoration)

Instructions:

1. Start by preparing the sweet red bean paste (anko) if you're making it from scratch, or use store-bought if preferred.
2. In a mixing bowl, combine the mochiko and granulated sugar. Mix well.
3. Gradually add water to the mochiko mixture, stirring constantly, until a smooth dough forms.
4. Transfer the dough to a heatproof dish or bowl suitable for steaming.
5. Steam the dough over boiling water for about 20-25 minutes, or until it's cooked through and becomes translucent.
6. Once cooked, remove the dish from the steamer and let the mochi cool slightly.
7. Dust a clean work surface with potato starch or cornstarch to prevent sticking.
8. Transfer the warm mochi onto the dusted surface.
9. Divide the mochi into equal portions and shape each portion into a small disk.
10. Place a small amount of sweet red bean paste (anko) in the center of each mochi disk.

11. Fold the edges of the mochi over the red bean paste to enclose it completely, shaping it into a ball or oval.
12. Wrap each filled mochi with a pickled cherry blossom leaf (sakura leaf), placing the leaf with the glossy side facing outwards.
13. Optionally, decorate the Hanabiramochi with edible gold or silver leaf for a touch of elegance.
14. Serve the Hanabiramochi as a delightful Japanese sweet treat, and enjoy the springtime flavors!

Hanabiramochi is not only delicious but also visually appealing with its vibrant colors and delicate cherry blossom leaf decoration. It's perfect for celebrating the arrival of spring or for enjoying during cherry blossom viewing parties (hanami).

Kusa Mochi (Grass-flavored Rice Cake)

Ingredients:

- 200g (about 1 1/4 cups) mochiko (glutinous rice flour)
- 100g (about 1/2 cup) granulated sugar
- 200ml (about 3/4 cup plus 2 tablespoons) water
- 100g (about 3.5 oz) fresh yomogi leaves (Japanese mugwort leaves), washed and finely chopped
- Potato starch or cornstarch, for dusting

Instructions:

1. In a mixing bowl, combine the mochiko and granulated sugar. Mix well.
2. In a blender or food processor, blend the chopped yomogi leaves with water until smooth.
3. Strain the yomogi mixture through a fine-mesh sieve to remove any solid bits. You should have about 200ml of yomogi liquid.
4. Gradually add the yomogi liquid to the mochiko mixture, stirring continuously to form a smooth batter.
5. Transfer the batter to a heatproof dish or bowl suitable for steaming.
6. Steam the batter over boiling water for about 30-40 minutes, or until it's cooked through and becomes slightly translucent.
7. Once cooked, remove the dish from the steamer and let the mochi cool slightly.
8. Dust a clean work surface with potato starch or cornstarch to prevent sticking.
9. Transfer the warm mochi onto the dusted surface.
10. Divide the mochi into equal portions and shape each portion into a ball or disk.
11. Serve the Kusa Mochi immediately, or let it cool completely before serving.

Kusa Mochi is a delightful Japanese sweet with a unique green color and earthy flavor from the yomogi leaves. Enjoy it as a snack or dessert with a cup of green tea, or alongside other traditional Japanese sweets. Store any leftovers in an airtight container at room temperature for up to several days.

Wasanbon (Refined Japanese Sugar)

Ingredients:

- 100g (about 1 cup) warabi starch (bracken starch)
- 2 cups water
- 50g (about 1/4 cup) granulated sugar
- 1 tablespoon matcha powder (green tea powder)
- Kinako (roasted soybean flour), for dusting
- Kuromitsu (black sugar syrup), for drizzling (optional)

Instructions:

1. In a mixing bowl, dissolve the matcha powder in a small amount of water to create a smooth paste.
2. In a saucepan, combine the warabi starch and granulated sugar. Gradually add the remaining water while stirring to prevent lumps.
3. Place the saucepan over medium heat and cook the mixture, stirring constantly, until it thickens and becomes translucent. This should take about 5-7 minutes.
4. Once the mixture has thickened, remove it from the heat and quickly stir in the matcha paste until well combined.
5. Pour the mixture into a shallow dish or mold lined with plastic wrap. Smooth the surface with a spatula.
6. Let the mixture cool and set at room temperature for about 1-2 hours, or until firm.
7. Once set, remove the mochi from the dish or mold and cut it into bite-sized pieces.
8. Dust the Matcha Warabi Mochi with kinako (roasted soybean flour) before serving.
9. Optionally, drizzle with kuromitsu (black sugar syrup) for added sweetness.
10. Serve and enjoy the Matcha Warabi Mochi as a delightful Japanese sweet treat!

This Matcha Warabi Mochi recipe yields a delicate and slightly chewy texture with a rich matcha flavor, perfect for enjoying alongside a cup of green tea or as a sweet snack anytime. Adjust the sweetness and matcha intensity according to your taste preferences.

Kinako Warabi Mochi (Roasted Soybean Flour Bracken Starch Dumplings)

Ingredients:

- 100g (about 1 cup) warabi starch (bracken starch)
- 2 cups water
- 50g (about 1/4 cup) granulated sugar
- Kinako (roasted soybean flour), for dusting
- Kuromitsu (black sugar syrup), for drizzling (optional)

Instructions:

1. In a saucepan, combine the warabi starch and granulated sugar. Gradually add the water while stirring to prevent lumps.
2. Place the saucepan over medium heat and cook the mixture, stirring constantly, until it thickens and becomes translucent. This should take about 5-7 minutes.
3. Once the mixture has thickened, remove it from the heat.
4. Pour the mixture into a shallow dish or mold lined with plastic wrap. Smooth the surface with a spatula.
5. Let the mixture cool and set at room temperature for about 1-2 hours, or until firm.
6. Once set, remove the mochi from the dish or mold and cut it into bite-sized pieces.
7. Dust the Kinako Warabi Mochi with kinako (roasted soybean flour) before serving.
8. Optionally, drizzle with kuromitsu (black sugar syrup) for added sweetness.
9. Serve and enjoy the Kinako Warabi Mochi as a delightful Japanese sweet treat!

This Kinako Warabi Mochi recipe yields a delicate and slightly chewy texture with a nutty flavor from the roasted soybean flour. It's perfect for enjoying alongside a cup of green tea or as a sweet snack anytime. Adjust the sweetness according to your taste preferences.

Kusa Dango (Grass-flavored Dumplings)

Ingredients:

- 100g (about 3/4 cup) mochiko (glutinous rice flour)
- 50g (about 1/4 cup) granulated sugar
- 100g (about 3.5 oz) fresh yomogi leaves (Japanese mugwort leaves), washed and finely chopped
- Water, as needed
- Shiratamako (extra glutinous rice flour) or cornstarch, for dusting

Instructions:

1. In a mixing bowl, combine the mochiko, granulated sugar, and chopped yomogi leaves. Mix well.
2. Gradually add water to the mixture, stirring continuously, until a smooth dough forms. The dough should be firm but pliable.
3. Divide the dough into equal portions and shape each portion into a small ball or cylinder.
4. Bring a pot of water to a boil over medium heat. Drop the dango into the boiling water and cook until they float to the surface, about 2-3 minutes.
5. Once the dango float, continue to cook for another 1-2 minutes, then remove them from the water with a slotted spoon and transfer them to a bowl of cold water to cool.
6. Once cooled, drain the dango and dust them lightly with shiratamako or cornstarch to prevent sticking.
7. Serve the Kusa Dango on skewers or in small dishes, and enjoy them as a delightful Japanese sweet treat!

Kusa Dango have a subtle herbal flavor from the yomogi leaves and a chewy texture from the glutinous rice flour. They are often enjoyed with a sweet soy sauce glaze or dipped in kinako (roasted soybean flour) for extra flavor. Feel free to experiment with different variations and serving options to suit your taste preferences.

Yuzu Marmalade

Ingredients:

- 4-5 yuzu fruits
- 2 cups granulated sugar
- 2 cups water

Instructions:

1. Wash the yuzu fruits thoroughly under running water to remove any dirt or wax.
2. Using a sharp knife, cut the yuzu fruits in half horizontally. Remove any seeds with a spoon and discard them.
3. Slice the yuzu halves thinly, crosswise, into thin rounds. If you prefer chunkier marmalade, you can cut them into thicker slices.
4. In a large pot, combine the sliced yuzu fruits, granulated sugar, and water. Stir well to combine.
5. Place the pot over medium heat and bring the mixture to a boil, stirring occasionally to dissolve the sugar.
6. Once the mixture comes to a boil, reduce the heat to low and let it simmer gently for about 1-1.5 hours, or until the yuzu rinds are soft and translucent and the mixture has thickened to your desired consistency. Stir occasionally to prevent sticking.
7. As the marmalade cooks, skim off any foam that forms on the surface with a spoon and discard it.
8. Once the marmalade has reached the desired thickness, remove the pot from the heat and let it cool slightly.
9. Carefully transfer the hot marmalade into clean, sterilized jars, leaving about 1/4 inch of headspace at the top of each jar.
10. Seal the jars tightly with lids and let them cool to room temperature. As the marmalade cools, the lids should seal with a "pop" sound, indicating that they are properly sealed.
11. Store the sealed jars of yuzu marmalade in a cool, dark place for up to several months. Once opened, refrigerate the marmalade and consume it within a few weeks.
12. Enjoy your homemade yuzu marmalade on toast, scones, yogurt, or as a flavorful addition to sauces and marinades!

Yuzu marmalade is a versatile condiment with a bright citrus flavor and a delightful aroma. Experiment with different variations by adding herbs like thyme or spices like ginger for extra complexity.

Akafuku Mochi (Red Bean Paste-covered Rice Cake)

Ingredients:

For the rice cake:

- 1 cup mochiko (glutinous rice flour)
- 1/4 cup sugar
- 3/4 cup water

For the red bean paste:

- 1 cup cooked red beans (azuki beans)
- 1/2 cup sugar
- 2 tablespoons water

Instructions:

1. Prepare the red bean paste: If you're using canned red beans, drain and rinse them. If you're using dried beans, cook them according to the package instructions until they're soft. Then, mash or puree the cooked beans until smooth.
2. In a saucepan, combine the mashed red beans, sugar, and water. Cook over medium heat, stirring constantly, until the mixture thickens into a paste-like consistency. Remove from heat and let it cool completely.
3. In a microwave-safe bowl, combine the mochiko and sugar. Gradually add water while stirring until the mixture is smooth.
4. Cover the bowl with plastic wrap and microwave on high for 2 minutes. Remove from microwave and stir well. Return to microwave and cook for another 1-2 minutes, or until the mixture becomes translucent and sticky.
5. Dust a clean surface with potato starch or cornstarch to prevent sticking. Transfer the cooked mochi dough onto the dusted surface and knead it gently until smooth.
6. Divide the mochi dough into small portions and flatten each portion into a disc shape.
7. Place a small amount of red bean paste in the center of each mochi disc.

8. Gather the edges of the mochi disc and pinch them together to seal the red bean paste inside. Roll the mochi ball between your palms to shape it into a smooth ball.
9. Repeat the process with the remaining mochi dough and red bean paste.
10. Serve the Akafuku mochi immediately, or store them in an airtight container in the refrigerator for up to 2-3 days.

Enjoy your homemade Akafuku mochi!

Mizuame (Sweet Rice Syrup)

Ingredients:

- 1 cup glutinous rice flour (mochiko)
- 2 cups water
- 1 cup sugar
- 1 tablespoon rice vinegar or lemon juice (optional, for acidity)

Instructions:

1. In a saucepan, combine the glutinous rice flour and water. Stir well to dissolve any lumps.
2. Heat the mixture over medium heat, stirring constantly to prevent burning.
3. Once the mixture begins to thicken, reduce the heat to low and continue cooking, stirring frequently, until it reaches a thick, glue-like consistency. This may take around 20-30 minutes.
4. Add the sugar to the mixture and continue stirring until the sugar is fully dissolved.
5. If using rice vinegar or lemon juice, add it to the mixture and stir well. This helps to prevent crystallization and gives the Mizuame a smoother texture.
6. Continue cooking the mixture over low heat, stirring frequently, until it thickens further and reaches a syrupy consistency. This may take another 20-30 minutes.
7. Once the Mizuame has reached the desired consistency, remove it from heat and let it cool slightly.
8. Transfer the Mizuame to a clean, airtight container and let it cool completely before using or storing.
9. Store the Mizuame in the refrigerator for up to several weeks. It will thicken further as it cools.

Mizuame can be used as a sweetener in various recipes, such as traditional Japanese wagashi (sweets), sauces, glazes, or as a topping for desserts like shaved ice or pancakes. Enjoy experimenting with this versatile sweet rice syrup in your cooking!

Kudzu Mochi (Arrowroot Starch Cake)

Ingredients:

- 1 cup kudzu root starch (kuzu-ko)
- 1 1/2 cups water
- 1/4 cup sugar (adjust to taste)
- Kinako (roasted soybean flour), for dusting
- Kuromitsu (brown sugar syrup), for drizzling (optional)

Instructions:

1. In a saucepan, combine the kudzu root starch and water. Stir well to dissolve any lumps.
2. Place the saucepan over medium heat and cook the mixture, stirring constantly, until it thickens and becomes translucent. This should take about 5-7 minutes.
3. Add the sugar to the mixture and continue cooking, stirring constantly, until the sugar is fully dissolved and the mixture thickens further. This should take another 2-3 minutes.
4. Once the mixture reaches a thick, pudding-like consistency, remove it from heat.
5. Prepare a tray or shallow dish by lightly greasing it or lining it with parchment paper.
6. Pour the hot kudzu mixture into the prepared tray or dish, spreading it out evenly with a spatula.
7. Let the kudzu mochi cool and set at room temperature for about 30 minutes to an hour, or until firm.
8. Once the kudzu mochi has set, use a knife or cookie cutter to cut it into desired shapes.
9. Dust the cut kudzu mochi with kinako (roasted soybean flour) before serving.
10. Optionally, drizzle some kuromitsu (brown sugar syrup) over the kudzu mochi for added sweetness and flavor.
11. Serve the kudzu mochi as a delicious snack or dessert.

Enjoy your homemade kudzu mochi!

Yomogi Dango (Japanese Mugwort Dumplings)

Ingredients:

- 1 cup mochiko (glutinous rice flour)
- 1/4 cup sugar
- 1/2 cup yomogi leaves (fresh or frozen), finely chopped
- Water, as needed
- Kinako (roasted soybean flour), for dusting (optional)
- Anko (sweet red bean paste), for filling (optional)

Instructions:

1. If using fresh yomogi leaves, wash them thoroughly and remove any tough stems. If using frozen yomogi leaves, thaw them according to package instructions.
2. In a mixing bowl, combine the mochiko, sugar, and chopped yomogi leaves.
3. Gradually add water to the mixture, stirring continuously, until it forms a smooth and pliable dough. The amount of water needed may vary depending on the moisture content of the yomogi leaves.
4. Once the dough comes together, divide it into small portions and roll each portion into a ball, about 1 inch in diameter.
5. If you'd like to fill the dumplings with anko (sweet red bean paste), flatten each dough ball slightly and place a small amount of anko in the center. Fold the dough over the filling and roll it back into a ball, ensuring the filling is completely enclosed.
6. Bring a pot of water to a boil. Drop the dough balls into the boiling water in batches, being careful not to overcrowd the pot. Cook the dumplings until they float to the surface, which should take about 2-3 minutes.
7. Once the dumplings are cooked, remove them from the water using a slotted spoon and transfer them to a bowl of cold water to cool briefly. This helps to firm up the dumplings and stop the cooking process.
8. Drain the dumplings and skewer them onto wooden skewers if desired.
9. Optional step: Dust the skewered dumplings with kinako (roasted soybean flour) for added flavor and texture.
10. Serve the yomogi dango as a delicious snack or dessert.

Enjoy your homemade yomogi dango!

Kibi Dango (Millet Dumplings)

Ingredients:

- 1 cup kibi (millet) flour
- 1/4 cup sugar
- Water, as needed
- Kinako (roasted soybean flour), for dusting (optional)
- Anko (sweet red bean paste), for filling (optional)

Instructions:

1. In a mixing bowl, combine the kibi flour and sugar.
2. Gradually add water to the mixture, stirring continuously, until it forms a smooth and pliable dough. The amount of water needed may vary depending on the texture of the flour.
3. Once the dough comes together, divide it into small portions and roll each portion into a ball, about 1 inch in diameter.
4. If you'd like to fill the dumplings with anko (sweet red bean paste), flatten each dough ball slightly and place a small amount of anko in the center. Fold the dough over the filling and roll it back into a ball, ensuring the filling is completely enclosed.
5. Bring a pot of water to a boil. Drop the dough balls into the boiling water in batches, being careful not to overcrowd the pot. Cook the dumplings until they float to the surface, which should take about 2-3 minutes.
6. Once the dumplings are cooked, remove them from the water using a slotted spoon and transfer them to a bowl of cold water to cool briefly. This helps to firm up the dumplings and stop the cooking process.
7. Drain the dumplings and skewer them onto wooden skewers if desired.
8. Optional step: Dust the skewered dumplings with kinako (roasted soybean flour) for added flavor and texture.
9. Serve the kibi dango as a delicious snack or dessert.

Enjoy your homemade kibi dango!

Amazake Ice Cream

Ingredients:

- 2 cups heavy cream
- 1 cup whole milk
- 3/4 cup sugar
- 1/2 cup amazake
- Pinch of salt

Instructions:

1. In a saucepan, combine the heavy cream, whole milk, and sugar. Heat the mixture over medium heat, stirring occasionally, until the sugar is fully dissolved and the mixture is warm.
2. Remove the saucepan from heat and stir in the amazake and a pinch of salt. Mix well to combine.
3. Pour the mixture into a bowl and let it cool to room temperature. Once cooled, cover the bowl with plastic wrap and refrigerate for at least 4 hours or overnight to chill completely.
4. Once the mixture is chilled, pour it into an ice cream maker and churn according to the manufacturer's instructions until it reaches a soft-serve consistency.
5. Transfer the churned ice cream to a freezer-safe container and freeze for an additional 2-4 hours, or until firm.
6. Before serving, let the amazake ice cream sit at room temperature for a few minutes to soften slightly. Scoop into bowls or cones and enjoy!
7. Optionally, garnish the ice cream with toppings such as fresh fruit, toasted nuts, or a drizzle of amazake for extra flavor.
8. Store any leftover amazake ice cream in the freezer in an airtight container for up to several weeks.

Enjoy your homemade amazake ice cream as a delicious and unique dessert!

www.ingramcontent.com/pod-product-compliance
Lightning Source LLC
LaVergne TN
LVHW081617060526
838201LV00054B/2283